Previous Books (in English)

Darkening Mirror: New and Selected Poems, Wang Jiaxin, Edited and Translated by Diana Shi and George O'Connell, Foreword by Robert Hass, Tebot Bach, 2017.

At the Same Time

New and Selected Poems

ARROWSMITH
PRESS

At the Same Time
New and Selected Poems
Wang Jiaxin

ISBN: 979-8-9915254-6-6

Library of Congress Control Number: 2025914187

Boston — New York — San Francisco — Baghdad
San Juan — Kyiv — Istanbul — Santiago, Chile
Beijing — Paris — London — Cairo — Madrid
Milan — Melbourne — Jerusalem — Darfur

11 Chestnut St.
Medford, MA 02155

arrowsmithpress@gmail.com
www.arrowsmithpress.com

Cover Art: Shang Yang, The Remaining Mountains-6, 2014.

The seventy-first Arrowsmith book was typeset & designed by
Gerard Robertson for Askold Melnyczuk & Alex Johnson in Garamond Font

At the Same Time

New and Selected Poems

Wang Jiaxin

Translated from Chinese by John Balcom

More Praise for *At the Same Time*

In an age when words are too often fog banks, *At the Same Time* brings the happiness of the real thing. Each poem opens thought, eyes, and heart. Each poem carries discovery. Wang Jiaxin's many dialogs with the great poets and philosophers carry his own distinctive vision, perspective, compassion, and authority: a bedrock looking and saying. A world poet comes into English in these powerful poems' translations. I can't commend it highly enough to readers' attention.

—Jane Hirshfield

At the Same Time gathers some of best poems by Wang Jiaxin, a major voice of contemporary Chinese poetry. Together these poems show a mature mind, a distinct voice, a peculiar eye, a broad vision and above all, a genuine spirit.

—Ha Jin

If we agree with Charles Simic that the secret wish of all lyric poetry is to stop time, Wang Jiaxin is certainly a man whose wishes had been answered—a remarkable achievement in this day and age. This ongoing conversation with the larger world in the timeless moment is what draws me to Wang Jiaxin's poems. A soul might be a synonym for solitude, but herein the soul is in conversation, a beautiful thing of lyric inquiry—for which I am most grateful.

—Ilya Kaminsky

A rare thing happened as I read Wang Jiaxin's poems: I felt stirred to write poems. I don't know much about his experience, but for me it's a sign of some unusual force in the poems I'm reading. In these compressed lyric poems, in poem after poem, I felt that flash of perception, that transformation of the literal into the revealed, even the metaphysical. And the startlement of recognizing, oh! Here's evidence of intelligent life on earth.

—Rosanna Warren

Acknowledgments

Grateful acknowledgment is made to the following publications where some of these translations have previously appeared in print:

Arrowsmith: "After Kobayashi Issa," "At the Same Time," "For Imre Kertész," "In the Native Place of Laozi," "Joseph Brodsky on Cape Cod," "Last Year's Snow," "Remembering 11 White Temple Hutong in Xidan," "Someone," "The Great Poets in Sad Times," "To W. H. Auden,"and "Untitled."

Chinese Literature and Thought Today: "Snow Poem," "Farewell," "A Tree on Santorini," "Flight," "February," "An Osmanthus Tree," "On the Ferry," and "Dandelions: In Arthur Sze's Garden."

Five Points: "Drinking with His Son."

Free Verse: "Pastoral Poem."

Hanging Loose: "For a Future Reader," "Hart Crane's Piano," "Imre Kertész," "At Dongtou," "At Du Fu's Thatched Cottage," and "A Dish of Peaches in Russia."

Washington Square Review: "At Weihai, Someone Asks Me about the Poet Duo Duo," and "Homage To."

The Hopkins Review: "Gwangju Boy" (online) and "Flight Path" (print).

A Century of Modern Chinese Poetry: An Anthology, edited by Michelle Yeh, Zhangbin Li, and Frank Stewart. Seattle: University of Washington Press, 2023: "Oranges," and "Pasternak."

Push Open the Window: Contemporary Poetry from China, edited by Qingping Wang, Sylvia Lin, and Howard Goldblatt. Port Townsend: Copper Canyon Press, 2011: "Drinking with His Son," and "Pastoral Poem."

I met Wang Jiaxin in Beijing in 1990 and visited his house in White Temple Hutong on a number of occasions. Back then it functioned as a kind of salon for poets visiting Beijing from other parts of China. Everyone referred to the three kingdoms of poetry in those days — Beijing, Nanjing, and Chengdu. It was also an unsettled time of uncertainty. After 1990 we didn't see each other again for many years. Late that year he wrote the poem "Pasternak", one of his most influential and oft-quoted works, post-89. Subsequently, I followed his career and translated some of his poems. Tested by history, he is a poet who has replied with ever more strength and assurance. We reconnected when he came to the States to accompany his son, a student here. When Wang suggested the present volume, I naturally jumped at the chance. I am grateful for his active interest in the translation process. Discussing the translations with such an accomplished poet and translator has been one of the more enjoyable experiences I've had as a translator. I have always felt a great affinity for his work and hope that comes across in these versions.

The translator and the author would also like to thank Arthur Sze for generously taking time to read the manuscript and offer suggestion as well as for his advice in general.

I would like to dedicate this translation to the memory of my beloved wife Yingtsih.

John Balcom

CONTENTS

This Street (2016-2020)

At the Same Time (2021-2024)

For a Future Reader (1990-2016)

My Flight Path (2024-2025)

This Street

(2016-2020)

This Street

I shall not return my borrowed dust
To the earth...
—Osip Mandelstam

1

After many tumultuous years of life,
I too live on a street, a small street in a residential area,
A shady green street where we have lived now for five years,
One that still awaits the swallows of my childhood
And a butterfly from Mandelstam.

2

Every day I go down to the street at golden dusk,
Or at green noon accompanied by singing cicadas,
Even when I'm writing I can't resist
Looking out at the street, as if it's the indispensable
Blank space between two lines of verse.

3

A girl in a short skirt is walking by right now, and how I wish
Her lithe movements were still
Like the eternal figure on that Grecian urn,
At least she could slow down so that I might
        glance at her for old Du Fu,
Or offer her a hand for Yeats.

4

On this street I buy my daily bread and vegetables...
(Sometimes I go out just for something to feed our rabbit)

Oh, the steam that rises from the pots at the dumpling place!
And the kindergarten, how I like the joyful cries of the kids as much as
The silence after school lets out: the eternal silence of childhood.

5

Unforgettable spring (What year was that?) one step beyond
The iron fence and the peach trees blossom,
Dreamlike, albeit for three days,
Then several clouds drift before my captive eyes,
Just drifting, even on a blighting smoggy day.

6

The squatting mechanic,
        the fleet delivery person,
                the guy handing out flyers...
I salute you all, and not only that but
Every year noisy funeral processions go down the street,
When that happens, I take my son to the window,
As if it were to see the other side of the moon.

7

Toward nightfall, you can smell the aroma of roasting
        sweet potatoes on the street,
("Paris no longer eats chestnuts in the streets," wrote Eluard*)
Noon, the shadows of the power poles lengthen.
Early summer, the tender yellow flowers of the
        old locust tree carpet the ground,
After autumn rains, the gold coin of the gingko tree!

8

Sometimes I write for days without going downstairs,
But the street is still there, pulling open the curtains,
        ah, the snow is falling!
At that moment, it's as if Heaven is there to deliver us!
At that moment, I and even our little rabbit
Stand stock still at the window for a long time.

9

This street isn't really our home,
We rent here for our kid's school,
But I love this street, the fourth-floor window,
        (neither too high nor too low),
I love the four seasons on the street, the light and shadow,
It has already colored my soul.

10

And the breeze on the street! Every time I go out
        as if sleepwalking,
It gently greets my brow with a caress.
Many times it has reconciled me with life. On muggy days
It seems to carry me away to Qingdao or Dalian--
Turn the corner and there are the sea and the sails!

11

Yes, I love this street because it made me settle down,
It made me live again with this "borrowed dust".
On the night of my birthday, I wished to keep walking down it,
The street is less than 500 meters, so I walked it there and back thrice
Accompanied by a little star that brought tears to my eyes.

12

And I love this street because I have a view of the mountains
(fortunately not entirely blocked by high-rises) -- Beijing's Xishan,
I love its black silhouette against the flare of dusk,
I love the first bright headlights at the far end of the street
As if they were driving toward me from the margins of the soul.

13

It's just a nameless little street (you'd never find it by reading this
poem),
Living here, I translated Mandelstam,
He had no fixed residence, died in exile, but hoped after death
That a "white butterfly" might live out its span--
To fly back to that country, to fly back to that street.

14

And "that street" is "this street", just as
"This street" will become "that street"--
Next year after our child finishes primary school, we'll move,
But years later I will revisit it, as will our child--
Perhaps the swallows of my childhood will come with him.

August 2016
Beijing Century City

*From the poem "Courage" by Paul Eluard.

From Akhmatova's Window

In St Petersburg,
At the Anna Akhmatova Museum,
On the fourth floor of the "Fountain House"*
As if traversing the fourth circle of hell,**
    and at mid-slope looking back--
I look out the window at the garden with its unlikely scenery,
I see a mythic harpy partially hidden among the trees,
I see a suffering mother, a defiant son, and a father
    knocked to the ground with the butt of a gun,***
I see a funeral melt amid the tree branches;
I see a lover from a past life still sitting dazed on a bench,
I see people papering the tree trunks with poetry;
I see people leaving, each making the sign of the cross,
I see Marina's****large sunken eyes staring at me;
I see people stealthily peeking from behind the trees,
Microphones in their pockets;
I see a blackbird hopping on the grass, followed by another;
I see the snow piled in one corner of the garden,
    still unmelted after so many years.
I see spirits of the dead still flagellating themselves.
I see summer in the trees and the approaching gold of autumn.
I see the most sorrowful circular dance on spring grass.
I see all of this, "as if bidding farewell again
To what I parted from long ago."*****
I see it all, as if dreaming with my eyes wide open.
I see it, I feel someone behind me at my right shoulder
Together with me, gazing into the distance
Because I climbed the tower of time, spiraling upward
To stand at Akhmatova's window.

       July 2016
       St. Petersburg

*The Fountain House is an 18th century Baroque palace with gardens built for the noble Sheremetev family. It was converted to an apartment building during the Soviet period. The poet lived for many years on the fourth floor of the Fountain House with the art historian Nikotay Punin.

**Dante's Inferno. Akhmatova wrote a number of poems about Dante and his Inferno.

***This line alludes to the tragic experiences of Akhamatova and her family. Her first husband, Nikolay Gumilev was executed for counter-revolutionary activities by the Soviet regime; their son Lev Gumilev was jailed in 1935 and again in 1938. While her son was imprisoned, Akhamatova wrote a series of poems titled "Requiem".

****Marina refers to Marina Tsvetaeva. After Tsvetaeva committed suicide in 1941, Akhmatova wrote a number of poems in memory of her.

*****Quoted from the "Introduction" of Akhmatova's long poem Poem without a Hero written in her later years. (translation by Judith Hemschemeyer).

At Weihai, Someone Asks Me about the Poet Duo Duo*

Strolling on the coast at Wehai, I gaze at a distant ship,
Someone asks me about the poet Duo Duo.
I say he has retired from Hainan University, but gets no pension,
Because "he is a foreigner."
"What does he live on? Is he invited to lecture?"
"He refuses. His pride, you know 'All of England cannot
Accommodate my pride...'"**
"Where is he staying in Beijing, then?" He rents a place,
(They tore down the place he inherited from his father.)
He writes poems there, reads Celan, reads Char, reads his
Penniless Tsvetaeva,
Sometimes he paints, but not for money...
"Hey, why is he called Duo Duo, ***or twice superfluous?
He's superfluous abroad and just as superfluous at home."
The poet Wang Guilin sighs, the rest of us force a smile;
I raise my head, and wonder where that
White ship on the sea has gone…

August 2017

*Duo Duo is the pen name Li Shizheng, a renowned contemporary poet born in Beijing in 1951. In 1969, he went to the Baiyang Lake Production Brigade, where he started writing poetry. In 1989, he went into exile abroad for more than ten years, becoming a citizen of Holland. Later he was hired by Hainan University as a foreign professor.

**Quoted from Duo Duo's poem In England.

***Duo Duo's name is composed of two duo (多)characters. The character duo(多)means superfluous.

From Zhangjiakou*

From Zhangjiakou, someone sent me
A box of canned mushrooms
Two skinned wild rabbits
And a big bag of potatoes.

I gave the rabbits to some relatives,
The potatoes I kept. But whenever I peel a potato,
I think of those two rabbits skinned bare
Hanging there...

I can only recall the lush Bashang Grasslands,**
For a little so-called comfort.

September 2017
Beijing

*Zhangjiakou is a city in northern Hebei province, located near the grasslands of Inner Mongolia.

**Bashang Grasslands or Bashang Plateau, is a vast expanse of natural grassland covering several thousand square miles in northern Hebei Province and Inner Mongolia.

A Bowl of Rice

In Pyeongchang*
A bowl of rice at noon
Rice, one bowl in the evening

Sometimes with doenjang soup
Sometimes with a plate of pickled vegetables

Or with a plate of minnows
Or with a few greasy perilla leaves

I've had to learn to sit cross-legged
My low dining table
My ebony bowl

Never have I paid so much attention
To a single thing as I do now

My chopsticks give thanks
My Adam's apple bobs

My inevitable previous life
A bowl of rice
My accidental afterlife
A bowl of rice

My begging monk in the distance
A bowl of rice
My brothers in jail
A bowl of rice

As if our lifetime of toil
Is just to bring us to a bowl of rice

The bowl is empty
The bowl is there

My journey, my rainy night
My green and yellow

My three thousand miles of sunlight
Here
Become a bowl of rice

September 2017
Pyeongchang, South Korea

*Pyeongchang, South Korea, was the host city of the 2018 Winter Olympics. Before the Olympic games, it hosted an international poetry festival.

In Your Room

In your room, no matter what pictures you hang
Be it of a horse, photos of the masters
Or even a sketch of St Petersburg
They all become your self portrait

And when you stroll down the street, no matter
What tree you see, or what person you run
Into, you're just one of them...
You have no reason to be proud

January 2018

Dawn, 5AM

Dawn, 5am, the insomniac is again at his desk.
The ashtray full of butts. The whole night spent chatting
      with ghosts. In the hallway
The sound of departing footsteps. If I can see it's because
I gradually floated out of a sea of suffering.
The first electric tram went by a century ago,
The bird nests are still filled with unhatched darkness.
Dawn, 5am, only the prisoners are outside to see
The smudge of pale blue appearing on the horizon,
Others struggled all night (like my mother), and finally
Stopped breathing, dawn, at 5am, on this
Boundary, wavering like a line on a cardiogram...

February 2018

28

Farewell

Yesterday evening, for one last time
I visited my parents' grave in the mountains
(In the end they were together again)
Then I went to see my aunt before leaving this morning
Now the plane roars, taking off from a new airport
Big as an aircraft carrier in the mountains of northwest Hubei
Flying to Shanghai

What a relief
It really feels like a burden has suddenly been lifted
Down below are the impoverished mountains of home
Snow lingers in the gullies and on the north-facing slopes
(The snow has melted on the sunny south-facing ones)
The gravel pit gouged in the mountain (like an exposed wound)
The blue reservoir is like a teardrop...

There are the mountains and rivers and kitchen smoke I know--
My father's white head and the fine wrinkles on mother's face...
The mountain road I trod to school as a youngster
The land where my childhood lies buried along with my relatives...
But this is the very first time I've seen it from the air
As my plane ascends, I continue trying
To recognize things down below
How I wish I was that boy who traveled on a goose*
And like him wipe away the tears one last time
And start a new life

February 2018

*An allusion to The Wonderful Adventures of Nils by Selma Lagerlöf.

Accompanying My Son to Sweep the Graves during the Qingming Festival*

Qingming Festival--
I accompany my son to sweep the graves,
For a bunny that died last year,
For a hamster that died the year before,
All buried in a quiet corner of the garden;
"They're buried here," my twelve-year old son squats,
I squat with him there.
No grave stone, no "endless drizzle",
Those once lively and energetic bodies,
Have long since decayed in the ground,
(The boys play basketball in the distance
The bouncing ball breaks the silence)
But I can still see their eyes
--dark eyes like black pearls,
Once they were in a metal cage,
Now, in the early spring air
They stare at me.

April 2017

*Qingming Festival, also known as Tomb Sweeping Festival (usually in early April), is a day the Chinese traditionally sweep the family graves and pay tribute to the dead.

A Legend

According to legend, owing to high winds and heavy seas
The sacred ceremony at which the Athenians offered
Sacrifices to Apollo at Delos was postponed
Therefore the execution of Socrates was also postponed
He was thrown into prison
His disciples took turns visiting him
And so we have the record of that dialogue*

What made you think of this?
Floating on the Aegean Sea
Time and prisoners
Flames and paper
Eyes and cutting wind...
Even the beauty of the calm sea
Is also amazing...
Then let that person continue talking--
Dedicating himself
To a pair of mortal lips.

October 2018
Greece

*The Phaedo is a Platonic dialogue, the philosophical subject of which is the immortality of the soul. It is set in the last hours before the death of Socrates.

A Tree on Santorini

On the island of Santorini
Is a tree
At dusk it fills with birds

Thank you, Athina
Thank you for showing me that tree

On the volcanic island of Santorini
It appears there is just the one tree
At dusk all the birds seem to
Wing their way there
As if it were their sole
Church

Many days have passed since I left
But every evening
I can still hear the chittering
Birds filling the tree at twilight
Unsure of whether it's out of joy
Or fear

Thank you, Athina
Thank you for showing me that tree

November 2018
Beijing

*Athina is a Greek artist living on Santorini.

In the Procession of Tears

Several years ago, Kubin called me:*
Wang, my friend, you know,
When I translated your "Pomelo" I cried,
I cried!

And today, in Venezuela,
Thousands of people flooded the streets,
While everyone else was shouting slogans,
A thirty-year-old woman just couldn't stop crying,
Crying, she kept up with the procession...

Don't ask why she is crying,
Don't ask!

Don't ask that German sinologist,
Don't ask the prisoner whose face is covered with tears,
Don't ask Du Fu...

O, poet, if you wish to be saved,
Then join that procession of tears--
O, the long poem of a long night,
A long night with no daybreak,
O, that torch of tears...

January 2019
Shanghai

*Wolfgang Kubin, a renowned German sinologist and translator, is a professor at the University of Bonn.

Hart Crane's Piano*

*—for Xu Yue***

In New York, just off the Brooklyn Bridge
In a corner of the "Poets House",
I saw a polished piano
That was yours back in the day.

It's true, you performed with language,
That immortal bridge rose from your playing
The arc of hope and despair, ambition and admiration,
From this shore to that, from Whitman
To your own ties and harmonies.

I haven't read much more of your poetry,
But I know your voice is still in the New York subway stations,
And still reverberates
In an empty Tsingtao beer bottle
Drained by a young Chinese poet.

But in the end what did you save?
Your piano is forever silent.
Some things can be heard only at the bottom of the sea.

February 2019

*Hart Crane (1899-1932), was a prominent American poet of the early 20th century. His representative work is the long poem The Bridge. On April 27, 1932, while returning to New York from Mexico by ship, he committed suicide by jumping overboard in the Gulf of Mexico. The last line alludes to this.

**Xu Yue, a young Chinese poet, is a translator of Hart Crane's poems.

In the Native Place of Laozi

Legend has it that Laozi was born an old man
Laozi had no childhood

No one but Confucius, who asked him about the rites
Knew who Laozi was

We climbed to Laojuntai, high up and precipitous
Twenty-five hundred years later

Living in troubled times, he went to Hangu Pass
Where he paid his 'toll' in full and left

Some say he became a crane
Others say he's held up in Denmark to this day--

Like Bertolt Brecht, listening to the howl
Of his old country over the radio*

While using a pen of no use to write
In his fortunate journal of exile

May 2019
Henan, Luyi, Zhoukou

*Bertolt Brecht was a German poet and dramatist. After the Nazi seizure of power, he went into exile. While in Denmark, he wrote the poem, "Legend of the Origin of the Book Tao Te Ching on Laotze's Road into Exile".

Chronicles of June

That year he was still a boy; after dying on the square
        he turned into a cricket,
And returned to the dark fields of his childhood.
Following which the fiery heat of the seventh month ebbed.*
Every July giant Mars hung to the west over our heads.
Followed by preparing warm clothes in the ninth month.*
        And his mom could only weep taking out
The shoes and socks he wore when he was little,
Along with some pitiful little plastic bowls.

That year, dawn didn't flow from star-like bullet holes.**

And now it's June again, I walk through the weeds of time,
        hearing a cricket,
I really want to say: "That's the one!"
But all I hear is the "Wow" in the wind...

June 2019
Beijing

*"The fiery heat of the seventh month ebbed" and "preparing warm clothes in the ninth month" are quoted from the poem "Seventh Month" in the Airs of Bin section of the Book of Poetry. The fiery heat ebbed refers to the planet Mars descending in the West; while "preparing warm clothes in the ninth month" refers to the time when women were tasked with sewing warm clothes. The two lines are well known and still recited in China today. Though quoted here, the meaning is not identical with the original.

**This line refers to Bei Dao's poem Declaration -- for Yu Luoke: "From the star-like bullet holes shall flow/A blood-red dawn." (Bonnie S. McDougall, trans).

Imre Kertész

From when you were sent to Auschwitz at fourteen
To Stockholm's glittering Concert Hall at seventy-three,
Your journey through life, Imre Kertész,
Has had a most unusual trajectory.

Is this an award for suffering?
No, this is "the victory of Auschwitz."
His lips twitched the way a dying man's
Twitch.

What else is there to say? Ah, dear earth,
Cruel earth,
Demonic earth,
Earth still belching smoke...

Then you bowed as if accepting the mercy of Death,
Or a gift from an enemy,
You received the prize from the hands of the king.

June 2019

*In commenting on being awarded the Nobel Prize, Imre Kertész said that
his work was nothing more than proof of "the victory of Auschwitz."

At Dongtou*

—for Wang Zigua, a young poet

When the body of a person** missing for years was dug
From the rocks in a middle-school athletic field,
Exposed to the oxidizing air,
We were talking poetry on a slope overlooking the sea.
Going over the differences and connections between two generations,
Discussing Zhang Zao*** and his "eternal sorrows" (Does it sound
More like doggerel today?)
Talking about that which was buried for years....
On the Dongtou peninsula in the East China Sea,
The sea scoured the granite again and again,
Booming in the cracks between our words.
Talking poetry as if nothing else happened.
Talking poetry as the fisherman on the reef
Cast his line even farther out.
Talking about the future, and the air we breathe, gradually
The rocks that weighed on the bones of the dead
Also began to weigh on our hearts.
Talking and talking, I suddenly recalled a line by Zhang Zao:
"Since life is a failure, why must poetry succeed?"
We sat in silence. All we could hear
Was the sound of the pounding waves.
Through our tears, we listened to the scouring of the sea.

June 2019

*Dongtou is a peninsula in Wenzhou, Zhejiang.

**Refers to a middle-school teacher in Huaihua City, Hunan. In 2003,
having revealed the corruption involved in the construction of the school's
athletic field, he was murdered and buried under the playground. The body
was found only in 2019 and reported by the media.

***Zhang Zhao (1962-2010), Chinese poet.

Wu Ningkun* in 1957

He grabbed a selection of Du Fu's poems and a copy of Hamlet,
Squeezed into a boxcar headed to a farm in the Great Northern Wilderness...

The two books proved to be his salvation during his hard life.
He didn't die (like so many of his friends in misery)
Because Du Fu could not die,
Much less the Prince of Denmark.

He did regret not bringing a copy of the Divine Comedy,
But even if Dante and his teacher Virgil had been there,
There'd be no telling what circle of hell they were in.
Would they lose their way? Would they be struggled against?
Digging in the frozen soil, gold stars still appeared before his eyes
With all his might, he shouted a name into the wind,
Bloated with hunger, he reeled and
Staggered, unable to keep up with the angels
Or match Satan's pace

June, 2019

*Wu Ningkun (1920-2019) was a famous Chinese translator and scholar of British and American literature. In 1957, during the Anti-Rightist Campaign, he was labelled an "extreme rightist" and sent to labor on a farm in the Great Northern Wilderness of Dongbei. He died in the United States in 2019. His memoir, A Single Tear (一滴泪), was published in the US.

Flight

My plane is flying
Like a slender dragonfly

From Moscow to Bucharest
My dragonfly has fifty pairs of eyes

And when passing through a cloud bank
My ears were blissfully deaf

Then come the colorful fields of Romania
Just like their national flag

If you're a deported prisoner
You can still see them chasing the tyrant on the road

If you are the returning Mihai Eminescu
You must prepare a poem for the crowds in the square

But I'm just a dragonfly
I fly, I look, and I seek

Nothing more on the ground than a single swaying stem
Of fragrant and dewy grass

November 2019

*Mihai Eminescu (1850-1889) was a Romanian Romantic poet.

To Mourn a Man

—for Dr. Li Wenliang (Oct 12, 1985-Feb 7, 2020)

In a neighborhood near the Jardin du Luxembourg
News of your passing came
My wife wept
Wept under the night sky of Paris

I didn't cry. But I couldn't sleep,
I searched my phone for any news,
Again and again I looked at that admonition to you:*
"Do you understand?"
"got it"
Till the final darkness came just before dawn...

And tonight, in Beijing I woke to the sound of rain,
(The weather report had predicted snow)
Lying in bed, listening to the rain,
I suddenly recall it's your "first seven",**
Are you back?

You are back. You never left,
You're still just as young.
The image of you in your black surgical mask rises again,
Your wide open eyes though surrounded by darkness
Look at all of us.

And the rain is still falling,
What way is this to mourn?
It's the first spring rain of 2020.

February 13, 2020
Beijing

*On January 3, 2020, Dr. Li Wenliang was admonished by the Wuhan police for posting warnings about the novel coronavirus (COVID-19) online. On February 7, Dr. Li died of COVID.

**The "first seven" refers to the first seven-day period after a person's death. On this day, people will hold memorial ceremonies for the dead.

41

February

"February. There's enough ink to weep."*
This line from Pasternak
Has been quoted a lot these days;
It's a line from a poem about happiness,
But it is circulating in an unfortunate time.

Night like iron.
(Someone seems to grope down the dark stairs.)
Eyes wide open, I lie in bed, as if bunked
In a ship's dark cabin, listening to
The steady snoring of my wife beside me,
It's what seems to
Push the ship forward
Through the long black night...

February 2020
Beijing, during the Covid lockdown

* This translation is based on the Chinese version by Xun Hongjun.

After Kobayashi Issa

We walk on the roof of hell
Gazing at flowers
—Kobayashi Issa

Sometimes we walk on the roof of hell
Gazing at flowers

Sometimes we walk on the edge of the flowers
Looking down into hell

I look out the window again now
Seeing nothing at all

How I long to return to the roof of my hell
Gazing at flowers

February 2020
Beijing, during the Covid lockdown

A Note

Shanshan is a girl from Wuhan, her parents were infected,
        her older brother was also infected,
Her mother departed, leaving behind the following note:

"Your cake flour was out-of-date, so I took it."
"Living on your own, buy small sizes, keep track of things."
"Not using something is the same as wasting it."
"You'll have to live frugally the rest of your life..."
"I won't nag anymore, this is the last time."

Reading this note, I burst into tears. I went downstairs.
I felt there is no need for us to write poetry.
Words are as heavy as mountains, not to be dragged.
How to get by in days to come, how to live carefully?
Up on Yueyang Tower*, Du Fu didn't know either.
To hear Heaven's exhortations, we need an orphan's ear.
We've written too much as it is.
Make poetry a last testament, bequeathing love in each word,
Only a mother in her final moments
Can do so.

> March 2020
> Beijing, during the Covid lockdown

*"Climbing up the Yueyang Tower" (登岳陽樓) is a poem written by Du Fu late in life.

The Death of a Beekeeper

The death of Lao She, *the death of Celan, the death of Mandelstam
The death of a doctor, the death of a nurse, the death of a doctor...**
Another death being the death of a beekeeper--
His name was Liu Decheng and he was from Xichang, Sichuan
Bright yellow rapeseed flowers covered the facing mountain slope
In the valley were black locust flowers, honeysuckle, and deeper in the mountains
The even more fragrant Chinese chastetree
But the road was blocked and red armbands were everywhere. He carried 176 beehives
Carrying his chorus of a different voice type("If you don't open
your mouth, you won't be able to speak anymore," said
the solitary singer to the others")
He went all over until he arrived at the border of two provinces
Unable to transition. The village chief he drank with didn't recognize him
Brandished a shovel, threatening to smash his beehives
As if crazy. After shouting a few final lines to
Startle Lao She and Shakespeare
He turned off his phone that was no longer charged
His chorus of bees became sporadic moans
His chorus of bees became a chill wind sweeping through the world
Becoming that final sound of mud
Falling on a coffin...
He died, he died in a tent no one dared enter
Died on the loneliest spring day--
Amid the lushest flower season he ever saw

February 2020
Beijing, during the Covid lockdown

*Lao She (1899-1966), a renowned modern Chinese writer. In 1966, during the Cultural Revolution, he took his own life by jumping in a Beijing lake after having been criticized and brutally beaten by the Red Guard.

**At the outbreak of COVID-19, many doctors and nurses died in the hospital after becoming infected.

Homage To

1

I pay homage to a Japanese monk,*
Because the teeth of a bream at the fish market
Made him feel a chill.

2

I can't see Lujia Mountain**, Mt.Fuji is even harder to see,
But a pot of jasmine blossoms at the window
Of my new place in August.

3

An evening stroll, it's like the road to Delphi.
Night in a dense wood,
Faint light on the river's surface.

4

He once praised the mystery and beauty of the peacock,
Now he avoids them,
As if they would come and feed on human flesh.

5

Language, and the rhythm of an aging body--
Greater hesitance and more pauses
And a request for greater calm.

6

Though cruel, I should thank your death:
The cold northern light of winter
In August reverts to us.

7

Six months after returning from the madhouse in St Remy,
He is still thinking of the blue irises Van Gogh painted--
That moment of silence penetrating the sandy land…

8

Shakespeare didn't know he was Shakespeare.
Du Fu said as he aged his poems became more easy-going.
The way it should be! Let's go out for a stroll.

August 2020
Wangjing, Beijing

*The Japanese monk referred to here is the haiku poet, Matsuo Basho. He
wrote a poem about how the sight of a bream's the teeth in the fish market
gave him a chill.

**Lujia Mountain is the site of the Wuhan University campus and is famed
for its cherry blossoms. In his youth, the author studied at Wuhan Univer-
sity.

Wild Chrysanthemums

I bought a large bouquet of chrysanthemums:
Purple, yellow, and pure white, I bought them quickly
As I came out of the supermarket yesterday evening
At a roadside flower stand
Before the two city inspectors got there

Today the flowers are in a vase
On my desk by the window
Decorating a poet's autumn

But where did the village woman selling the flowers go?
And the flatbed cart she clung to for dear life
Refusing to let the inspectors confiscate it?

I sink into my sofa, the wild chrysanthemums

Wilting before they fully bloom

September 2020
Beijing

An Osmanthus Tree

—for Dr. Li Zhijun

An exiled Russian poet* said, Judaism
Is like "a drop of musk filling a whole house",
I thought of these words as I opened the wooden
Gate of the Ruzhou Temple Academy**
And the blowing of osmanthus fragrance.

A small path through a bamboo forest. A pond of
        withered lotuses in early autumn.
A neglected garden, of many acres. A single osmanthus tree
Hidden among the weeds and other trees.
(You pointed it out to me)
Like a mountain landscape in ink. A breeze.
As if this were the only osmanthus tree in the world.
We strolled through the moonlit night,
        that faint fragrance our constant companion.
Like a wandering soul
All the way to the gate of Fengxue Temple on the mountain.
You talked about life's difficulties, about your years of pursuit,
You talked about abandoning the world and freedom that even
Your friends have a hard time understanding.
Yes, it all comes from that osmanthus tree down below
Its astringent and flowing fragrance
Which just happens to be our only religion.

                    September 2020
                    Ruzhou, Henan

*The exiled Russian poet referred to is Osip Mandelstam.

**Fengxue Temple Academy is located in the city of Ruzhou in Henan
Province.

Remembering 11 White Temple Hutong in Xidan

What number was it exactly? I can't seem to remember,
But Hai Zi* wrote it down in his address book,
I saw it written in black ink.
My family and I lived there for seven or eight years,
In the courtyard was a hundred-year-old date tree,
Two low buildings with gray tile roofs, on the ridges
Of which snails would appear after an autumn rain--
Duo Duo **put it all in a poem.
Our son grew up there.
Every year we "chopped wood for the winter".
We wept when we heard the tanks rumbling on the streets
Amid the pungent smell of gas...
Later, a monstrous bulldozer appeared,
Uprooting the old date tree,
Even the rib-like rafters were buried in the tile and rubble...
Today stuff is sold in the high-rise stores there,
No one knows a hutong once existed below.
For the living, the place held laughter, footsteps,
the soughing of the wind
And even the near silence of falling snow,
Preserved now only in the memories of one dead.

November 2020
Beijing

*Haizi (1964—1989), a contemporary poet. In 1979 he entered Beijing
University to study law.On March 26, 1989, he took his life by lying down
on railroad tracks near Shanhaiguan. After his death, his poetry had a
tremendous impact on a younger generation of Chinese.

**Duo Duo,a contemporary poet. He was born in Beijing in 1951 and is a
friend of the author.

At the Same Time

(2021-2024)

Marginalia, 2021

Du Fu in 2021

A number of poets today, just like parrots,
Fight and peck over a few grains of rice.
But from the big tree of my childhood,
A phoenix takes flight.

Bertolt Brecht

"No need to drive a nail into the wall"
--that's what Brecht said.
But we've already hammered in so many,
We've hung nothing on the wall
Other than a few dark holes.

Vermeer's Girl

Vermeer's little girl, many poets have praised
The pearl hanging from your ear,
But to me, its beauty,
The fusion of light and
Weight, is that it's really a teardrop

Marina Tsvetaeva

You died far from Moscow in the small town of Yelabuga,
But you still wander in the mountains of Czech Republic.
Even the birds can recite your poems.
But now you're tired, you want to sit and have a cigarette
But can you find anyone to give you a light?

The Street of Crocodiles

I haven't read Bruno Schultz's The Street of Crocodiles,
But I have seen that pair of wine-glass eyes
Feigning sleep.
Fortunately, the sunlight here is nice, the streets tidy,
        and the businesses open as usual,
Except for several remote-control garage doors
That are still closed.

Rereading The Gulag Archipelago

Barbed wire, code numbers, loudspeakers, searchlights...
Reading The Gulag Archipelago several years ago,
The stories of escaped prisoners fascinated me most;
Solzhenitsyn wrote them down
So that people might run away.
Are we still running now? Yes, still running.
Are we still running now? No, not any more.

2021
Beijing

At the Same Time

...at the same time, the Myanmar poet Khet Thi*
Was tortured in an interrogation room
His living organs were removed

At the same time, my wife's recently purchased pot
     of moth orchids blossomed
Swaying gently in the breeze

At the same time
I read the latest news online about a student who fell
     to his death at 49 High School in Chengdu
The official announcement is that "the family has no objection to the
     outcome of the inquiry"
And so died that young student

At the same time
I wanted to write a poem

No, I tore up that poem!

             May 2021
             Beijing

*Khet Thi, a Burmese poet, was killed during protests following the military coup of February 1, 2021 in Myanmar.

By the Fushui River I Think of Du Fu

On the banks of the Fushui River, where pike leap in swirling waters,
I can't help thinking of the poems you wrote here
About catching fish.*
How could a wandering poet at the end of his miserable life
Be so relaxed? No,
"The larger fish that are all wounded hang their heads,
Defiant in the mud and sand, sometimes they flop up straight."
Oh, it's like a massacre! Those large, protruding eyes,
The unspeakable pain,
Those shining fishing tridents, the flying kitchen knives,
Scared you, making you back away from the shore...
"From waves but a foot away they are forever lost!" Oh, what did you
see?
The little fish that escaped only to be trampled underfoot,
The bream still in the water, brighter than silver,
The carp leaping like taut bows in the nets,
They will struggle in your life from now on...
You never knew about "Ecological Conservation",
But you had to say goodbye to the surging Fushui River, to the
Carousing host and his lavish feast of fish--
You look up at the sky,
Then continue walking through this cruel land.

November 2020
Shihong, Suining, Sichuan Province

*Refers to two poems by Du Fu: Song of Watching Fishing and Watching
Fishing Again.

Testamentary Writing

Walking down the scorching streets of Moscow,
Osip turned to Anna and said:
"I'm ready to die."

Rimbaud said that every poem is the last.

And a sequence of my poems, before appearing in print
Was pulled from publication.

That's just as well. Thanks to fate I can still walk alone
On the outskirts of Beijing on such a beautiful autumn day.

Thanks to fate these words that are mortal
Need not become the last words for the future.

September 2021

"The Great Poets in Sad Times"

*—for the Kharkiv poet Serhiy Zhadan**

The great poets in sad times
Talk of hope
To keep their lines of defense from collapsing.
Nor does he give up his poetry, at least
He could share the art of song
With the darkling thrush alighted beside the trenches.

May 2022

*Serhiy Zhadan is a well-known contemporary Ukrainian poet and writer. He lives in Kharkiv and wrote a poem titled, "The Great Poet in Sad Times".

2022, Rereading Milosz

When Valery "counted verse syllables" at the noble Académie
Française,
Milosz said he was "busy elsewhere" (In occupied Warsaw?),
Where the searchlight swept, "his hair stood on end
His ear caught the screams of the hunt..."*

This is what sets him apart from his admired one-time master.
Pure poetry? That's just a dream. First he had to open his eyes:
"Machine gun fire in the streets made the cobblestones stand upright,
Like the quills of a porcupine..."**

April 2022

*See Milosz's late poem A Lecture translated by Czeslaw Milosz and Robert
Hass in Czeslaw Milosz, New and Collected Poems (1931-2001), New York:
Ecco, 2002.

* *See Milosz's Norton Lectures, The Witness of Poetry.

"For Paul Celan": The Anselm Kiefer Exhibition in Paris*

Wheelbarrows loaded with fire-blackened stone
A concentration camp in a glass case
A lead-gray canvas covered with huge scars
Brown bracken fern fronds stuck all over it

Paris, a large-scale installation in the Grand Palais Éphémère
A poet-painter who escaped from the
Smoking brick ovens of the Third Reich

Does he pay homage to Paul Celan?

The July air is hotter than ever
The ice in the Arctic Circle is melting
Here, the burning hot concrete avenues are filled with shadows
Drivers in line at a gas station in the distance swear
I turn my eyes away from a map of Ukraine
Filled with arched arrowheads of war
Black suns we cannot see burn in the sky above us

2022
Westbury, New York

*From December 2021 to January, 2022, the German artist Anselm Kiefer held a major art exhibition entitled "For Paul Celan" at the Grand Palais in Paris.

On Du Fu's Journey North*

On Du Fu's Journey North, did a fierce tiger
Really stand before him,
Splitting the gray cliff when it roared?

Years ago, I had my doubts, now I believe it.
Reality gives a poet
The right to imagine.

August, 2022

*In the second year of the An Lushan rebellion (757 AD), Du Fu
wrote his long poem Journey North (北征), in which he recounts
the hardships he experienced to visit home during the upheaval. The
poem contains the line: "A fierce tiger stood before me."

Last Year's Snow

The snow finally fell, it was last year's snow.
Making the room colder and darker.
Last year's snow finally fell today.

I've been through a lot of snowfalls,
But I feel that the snow falling in late February 2022
On the path of millions of fleeing Ukrainians
 Is the real snow,
Other snows are just vestiges.
It's the sort of snow that draws us to the window
To look farther into the distance.

January 2023
New York

The Boston Subway

—for Ha Jin

Head of white hair, made doubly hoary
By the frost and snow of northeast China
      and New England
In a dark corner of the Harvard Faculty Club
Shines radiantly

Your suit seems a little worse for wear
Just like the one Wunan* wore
To class after work

You led me out, eyes filled with the same
Excitement as thirty years ago, in search
Of the poetry bookstore in a corner of the campus

Then we said goodbye. I watched you disappear into
The entrance to the Boston subway --
Many years later, this brought to mind
The opening of Dante's Inferno

        March 2023
        Boston

*Wunan is the Chinese-American protagonist in Ha Jin's novel A Free
Life. He goes to school and writes poetry while also working in a Chinese
restaurant.

In Our Time

1

Men back from the front say:
In the trenches, it's hard to find anyone
Who refuses to pray.

2

"The Truth exists within a cannon's range"
This is a popular expression these days.
Poets without cannons, where is your truth?

3

In our time,
Some cannons have pretty flower names,
        "carnation" for instance...
While some concentration camps are hidden
In a fairyland of angelic birch trees.

4

A country as "united" as a "pomegranate"
A country composed of dozens of marshes
A country driven by tanks and "The Noseless Slut"*
A country in the dragon seat
A country controlled by the sorcery of soul-stealers
A country hanging, swaying from a tree's crooked neck
A country where prosthetics stock soars in value

5

He was released. The sack covering his head was removed.
He found himself in an open field in early autumn.
He could run to freedom with open arms.
What he didn't know, is that he had been left in
The middle of a beautiful --
filled with drifting golden leaves --
Minefield.

April 2023
New York

*The Noseless Slut--death. (The word for death in Russian is of feminine gender). See the third part of Anna Akhmatova's Poem without a Hero.

Joseph Brodsky on Cape Cod

In exile, Thomas Mann said where he was,
There was Germany,
Similarly, where Brodsky went, old Russia
Went too, for example, on Cape Cod in Massachusetts
He wrote: "The eastern tip of the Empire dives into night."*
(as if it were the shore of the Black Sea!)
Fortunately a mysterious cod came to visit him at night,
(his door was creaking)
Giving him another dream, an unearthly one,
A dream about hell, heaven, and Nothingness.

2023

*Joseph Brodsky, Cape Cod Lullaby, translated by Anthony Hecht, Collected Poems (New York: Knopf, 2023.)

To W. H. Auden

You once wrote an epitaph on a tyrant,
But you never realized
That was just one of his stand-ins.

2023
New York

At Du Fu's Thatched Cottage

—for Arthur Sze

We walked slowly beside the bamboo fence, I knew
You had traveled farther than me, thousands of miles farther

From the high-rises of New York where you were born, starting from
When your mother read you that first Tang poem

With no guide, we "let tears lead the way"
Relying on dimmer memories

We passed the pond, the colorful koi
Seemed to swim toward us out of a Song or Yuan painting

We walked through the lush bamboo grove, perhaps still
Growing from that same ancient rootstock

We had a photo taken in front the stone statue of the Poet-Sage
Your graying hair reflected in its greenish darkness

You seemed to want to say something but remained silent
You squeezed the hand of Carol, your wife
As if moving in a dream

We came to the three-room thatched cottage
Sat down on a block of stone by the door

We were silent, the thousand-year-old soul of poetry
Was also silent under the brooding gray sky

Perhaps only when the autumn wind rises
Lifting the thatch and sending it flying*

Will we once again hear that voice…

July 2023
Chengdu

*When Du Fu lived in Chengdu, he wrote a poem titled, "A Song on How My Thattched Roof Was Ruined by the Autumn Wind" (茅屋為秋風所破歌).

Someone

Someone talks too much, someone lives in silence

Someone says: "playing a violin in Auschwitz
is just like dancing on a corpse"

Someone's eyes burn in the dark
But are blinded by bright light

Someone writes disaster poems, others ask me to do so

Just like dancing on a corpse

Someone walks down the red carpet again, someone
Turns down a small path through the woods

Pine needles carpeting the ground, moister than our eyes

November 2023

"Breaking Bread"

—for Ilya Kaminsky and Katie Farris

You braved the cold and took the train from Princeton to New York
And invited me and my wife out to dinner

In a Chinese restaurant near Ukrainian Village we ordered
Plain boiled chicken, braised pork, glutinous rice cake,
      fried green beans, and mushroom fried rice...

And in your short message today I read: "It is so good
to have had the chance to break bread together"

Thank you, dear Ilya, for teaching me that
Wonderful expression: "breaking bread"

Yes, we didn't just simply eat, but "broke bread" together

We broke bread from Celan
We broke bread from Tsvetaeva
We broke bread from Chagall...

I still remember how you passed each dish to us

Yes, we passed the dishes to each other, with our eyes
And our poetry-writing hands
We "broke bread" together

At the same table

Under the watchful eyes of the spirits drawn around us

In a "Deaf Republic"*
Under red lanterns amid a hubbub of voices...

December 2023
New York

*Deaf Republic is a book of poetry by Ilya Kaminsky. It was translated into
Chinese by Wang Jiaxin and published in China in 2023.

On Long Island

(selections)

Sunny Day after Snow

Sunny day after snow. The distant church steeple covered in snow,
Clumps of grass with bits of icy debris along the road,
Steam rises from the Starbucks cup in my hands,
The coarse granules of rock salt stand
Like little guards scattered on the roadside,
And the final unuttered vowel in Lowell's poem*
All make me feel you -- a blast of a low icy wind from
The Atlantic Ocean...

Talking about the Russian Pianist Evgeny Kissin**

"He plays Bach and Chopin so well,
How could someone like him support war?"

"But Tolstoy's great-grandson
Is a fanatic supporter..."

Really? We said no more.
Again and again we listened to his early performance
Of Bach at the Tchaikovsky Concert Hall.
We sat down in the garden on a June evening,
Looking up, we saw risen
As if from blood and fire
The clear starry sky...

Can a Poem Be Finished?

Can a poem be finished?
Valery revised his poems countless times,
Always calling them simply "rough drafts",
Tsvetaeva said writing is rewriting;
And I've been in Long Island for two years,
Those old drafts still sit where I tossed them,
Not that I don't want to finish them,
Perhaps they are waiting for another hand.

2023
Westbury, New York

*Refers to the American poet Robert Lowell (1917-1977). He was born and spent a great deal of his life in Boston. On September 12, 1977, he died of a heart attack while riding in a cab in New York.

**Evgeny Kissin is a world famous pianist. Born in Russia, he now lives in London.

"A Dish of Peaches in Russia"

"A Dish of Peaches in Russia" is a poem by Wallace Stevens
I read when I was young; in the eyes of the American poet

They are large and round, they are red and fuzzy
They are full of juice, their skin thin and soft

They are filled with the village colors and
Fair weather, summer, dew, and peace

What a still-life painting! Accompanied by chapel bells
In a room where the curtains drift

But since Navalny was poisoned
Dare you touch this dish of Russian peaches?

They say by applying a little something called Novichok
The peaches will appear even redder and more alluring

Ah, to serve up such a dish of peaches
And serve them up again!

Ah, Russia, from now on I want only to tread your ice and snow
I want only to read the poems of your poets

Read Tsvetaeva and listen to why she says:
*No, no, I'm not a Russian poet**

Read Mandelstam and see how he blocks
That cone of light shooting from
The Admiralty spire**

Read Akhmatova: "We learned once and forever that
Blood only smells like blood…"***

Yes, all this smells like nothing else but blood!

> February 2024
> New York, upon hearing the news of Navalny's death.

*In a letter to Rilke from Marina Tsvetaeva.

**See Mandelstam's Voronezh Notebooks written while exile in Voronezh.

***See Akhmatova's poem Wild Honey Smells Like Freedom. Translated by Judith Hemeschemeyer.

On the Ferry

On the ferry from Staten Island to Manhattan
We pass the Statue of Liberty

Some people lean against the railing for a photo
Some sit in deck chairs to soak up the sun

She still holds high the bronze torch
But you no longer hear the call of those early years

In America, "freedom" has become an enigma
Something like money in Shakespeare

It lengthens the half-hour trip
Long enough to enact your life

It makes you look at the pursuing gulls for a long time
To see what in hell turns up in the ship's wake

March 2024
New York

Watching a Documentary*

Covering her ears, an old woman hid behind a broken wall
One artillery shell after another exploded
Making her tremble all over

Was it just proximity or by chance
That her shuddering shoulders were captured on film?

"You son-of-a-bitch..."
He actually even recorded several
Angry old men as they hurriedly fled
Curse him...

Are there any great documentarians? Perhaps.
According to Dante if you are to witness hell,
You have to be calm.

Or ask if you can control your fears,
For in those circumstances, your
Uncontrollably trembling limbs
Will hardly seem to be your own.

March 2024

*20 Days in Mariupol, which won the 2024 Academy Award for best documentary feature, was directed, shot, and produced in Ukraine.

Excerpted from a Memoir

At that time he was but a drop in a "sea of red"
So excited, he was on the verge of evaporating.
Amid the sound of the cheering throngs,
The leader stood on Tiananmen gate, leaning forward,
He waved his green military cap,
And shouted in his thick Hunan accent:
"Long...live...the...people..."

"Just like shooing flies." He thought back now,

And added these words.

April 2024

Total Solar Eclipse in North America on April 8, 2024

From Mexico City to Washington to Montreal
       to the northern hemisphere of our sore eyes,
The wonder of today's eclipse in North America
Brings to mind a line I once read by the Sichuan poet Ya Shi:
"Gravestones fly hugging the ground."

                  April 2024
                  New York

Desk

At the Mill Valley home of poet Jane Hirshfield
Is a long reddish-brown desk, clear finished

Is it made of pine? No, cherry wood

Ah, a cherry wood desk! Hard and fine-grained
Amber colored, a breath of the sun
The taste of mountain cherry, bitter and aromatic

It must have grown longer and harder than other woods

Put your hands on the desk, even without writing a word
Love is present for all trees, stone and air

I am envious. Though I want nothing, if I could
Have such a desk

The love it would evoke, would make us want
To wipe and caress it time and again with our hands

Like the world's shawl, slipping down
To reveal her shoulder blades, beautiful, bright, and firm

April 2024

In the Berkeley Hills

—for Cheng Baolin

April, on this lush, grassy slope stand old oaks
The spire of an Italian-style bell tower rises below, farther off
In the dazzling light of day stretches the
Bay, the freighters and the bridges....
We came up here to visit Czesław Milosz's old house,
But lingered longer on this nearby slope.
Perhaps the poet strolled here more than once
To gaze homeward and at his earlier days,
And what do I see? A girl in tennis shoes walking her dog
Passing in front of us, I watch her and her dog
Depart, disappearing down the hillside trail...
And to what do we "bear witness"? In this world evoking
Both despair and nostalgia, we are just passing through,
Passing through; perhaps that's all I can feel
A dog amid the fragrant grasses
Eagerly sniffing at a lingering scent.
All we can do is watch as things depart,
Always watching as something disappears.

April 2024
Berkeley

Dandelions: In Arthur Sze's Garden

In the beautiful
Santa Fe Foothills in New Mexico,
In the big garden of Arthur Sze, the Chinese American poet,
Were three old apple trees, sturdy and leafy,
A single willow tree, tall and lonely,
A row of cedars, and a recently flowered plum tree,
And several other flowers, the names of which escape me...
And beside a steaming hot-spring pool,
My host pointed and said, If you'd been here a month ago,
You could have seen the snow still covering the peaks...
Yes, I saw a lot,
I saw the clearest light falling through the tree leaves,
I saw how a young poet with a volume of Tang poetry
Came from Berkeley and took root here,
I also saw, in a grassy corner of the garden
Dandelions shaking in the wind, and they were
Nearly identical to those I saw in my childhood!
I really felt like crouching and asking them:
How are you doing here?
What wind carried you here?
Yes, what wind was it that crossed the ocean
And is still blowing in our ears?

May 2024
Santa Fe

Looking at Edward Hopper's Paintings

"American painter" "New England Painter"
"Realist painter"
After dispensing with these labels, we discover
That we are the people in your paintings

Be it sitting alone in a bar staring into his glass
Or opening a window that doesn't exist

A tranquil light
Like a sudden light
An echoing light
A light that brings delight
A fleeting light
A cold light, unsure if it's morning or evening
A light that makes you want to hold your shoulders
At last, this light
Shines on an empty bed...

May 2024

During Her Exile in Paris...

*

During her exile in Paris, Tsvetaeva said to Rilke:
No, I'm not a "Russian poet"

Why did she make such a claim?

The ten-plus letters she wrote to Rilke were all in German.
Only when she wrote poetry
Did she tearfully return to her Russian.

*

I met Gary Snyder once. He said he'd never cared
Anything about "The American Poetry Scene".
He said he was a "Pacific poet".

We were dining in a Vietnamese restaurant.
After a glass of beer, he said he liked Chinese Maotai,
A bit tipsy then, he narrowed his eyes--

Like a Japanese monk reborn? Or like Han Shan he translated
who has weathered the waves?

July 2024

Famine Years*

At that time we were not as hungry as the villagers around us
My parents were primary and middle-school teachers

I have no idea where my mother got an old hen
But, when she got home after class

Scattered over the floor, she found the uncooked
Legs and wings too tough to bite...

She gave me a beating, saying my crying
Had brought the neighbors over...

--I heard this many years later
I must have been four or five when it happened

I have no memory of it at all, but I do know
That little boy is still crying

I do know that his crying
Was weak and listless, but he is still crying

And amid the sound of his crying, I write
I know that behind his crying there is more crying

I know to this day no monument to those years
Stands on this land for us to bend down to

So I write and keep writing
I write amid all of that crying

October 2024

*Around 1962, millions of people died in a great famine in China.

For a Future Reader

(1990-2016)

Pasternak*

I can't leave a bouquet of flowers at your grave
But I am destined to pour my life into reading your poetry
With the passage through thousands of miles of driven snow
A shattered holiday, and the trembling of my soul

Finally able to write as one wants
But unable to live one's own life as desired
This is our common tragedy
Your lips grow more reticent, that's

The secret of fate, you cannot tell of it
You can only bear it, the scars deepening under your pen
For the sake of obtaining, you give up
For life, you demand your own death, to die completely

That is you, from one catastrophe to the next, you find me
You test me, making pain shoot abruptly through my life
From snow to snow, on a bus in Beijing rumbling through the mud
I read your poems, and in my heart

I shout the lofty names of those who were
Banished, sacrificed, and who bore witness, those
Souls who join together in a trembling mass
Those shining in death, and my own

Our own land! The shining tears in the northern livestock
The maple leaves burning in the wind
The darkness and hunger in the people's bellies, how
Can I ignore this just to talk about myself?

Like you, only by bearing fiercer blizzards
Can you defend your Russia, your
Larissa, **that beautiful, unbelievable miracle
Who can no longer be harmed

Covered with snowy coldness, there before your eyes!
And Levitan's candle-lit autumn
The death, praise, and sin in Pushkin's rhymes
Spring arrives, the vast land's blackness exposed

Open the soul toward all of this, poet
This is happiness, the highest law rising from the heart
Not suffering, it is ultimately what you bear
Ever unstoppable, coming in search of us

Seeking us, it demands symmetry
Or a requiem more vibrant than an echo
And us, how do we deserve to walk to your grave?
This is shame, this is December, winter in Beijing

This is the sadness in your eyes, seeking and questioning
Like a bell tolling, oppressing my soul
This is pain, this is happiness, to speak out about it
I need ice and snow to fill my whole life.

December 1990
Beijing

*This poem had a wide impact and has been seen as a sign that the poet had regained his voice after the historical events of 1989.

**Larissa is the female protagonist in Pasternak's novel Dr Zhivago.

Untitled

It doesn't start at the beginning of an era, but at the end
Inevitably a person comes walking toward you.
One who just might be a lover you haven't seen in years.

1995
Beijing

Pastoral Poem

If you wander the country roads outside the capital
You'll often see flocks of sheep
Spread out over the fields like patches of lingering snow
Like swollen buds bursting into bloom
Or, loudly herded, pressing together, crossing the road
Rolling down the ditch where the dust rises

I never really paid attention to them
Until I found myself driving behind a truck
On an afternoon as the snow was falling
I clearly saw their eyes that time
(And they were looking down at me)
So calm and so meek
As if oblivious to where they were being taken
Even treating my approach there
With a childlike curiosity

I slowed my car
I watched them
Vanish amid ever larger snowflakes

2004
Beijing

Oranges

That whole winter, he ate oranges,
Sometimes at the dinner table, sometimes on the bus,
Sometimes while he ate
Snow fell from inside, inside the bookcase;
Sometimes he didn't eat, just slowly peeled them,
As if something lived inside.

That's the way he ate oranges all winter,
While eating, he thought of the heroine in some
Novel, who carried a plate of oranges,
One of which kept rolling to the end of the story...
But he couldn't remember who wrote it.
He just ate oranges in silence.
The orange peels on his windowsill piled up.

He finally remembered the oranges
Placed by his hospital bed when he was a little boy,
He had no idea where his mom got them:
His little brother wanted to eat one, but his mom said no,
It was he who shared them with his brother;
But neither one of them could bear to eat the last one,
So there it remained on the nightstand.

(But what finally happened to that last orange?)

He ate oranges that way all winter long,
Especially on snowy days, or in gray weather:
He ate very slowly, as if
All he had was time,
As if he were swallowing darkness;
And so he peeled and ate oranges, looking up
The snowy radiance shined though his window.

2006

Drinking with His Son

What ambitions does a man past fifty still hold
His dream is but to sit and drink a glass of beer
With his long-estranged grown-up son
They clink their glasses together
This is the way they hug
It is also how they are reconciled
Then they say nothing
As the son gets up for another glass
The father stares blankly as the foam on the rim
Slips to the bottom of his glass

October 2007

Reading Lev Loseff's Biography of Joseph Brodsky*

From this book by an old friend of yours,
I learned that you liked Chinese food.
That you wrote only with ink.
I also learned that thirty years ago,
When I first read Pushkin,
You received a letter "from the Ming dynasty".**
I learned we were both born at the end of May,
Both in the sign of Gemini.
And your friend made me see more clearly
That star which shined only on you.
Genius, of course. I even seemed to be with Loseff
Listening to you give your first reading,
Your voice seemingly from beyond the clouds.
(To where you have since returned.)
The more I learned,
The sadder I felt for myself.
But, except for a gift of fire and ice
Prepared especially for you
By the Muse and Russia,
I also learned that the torture we have both suffered
Is one and the same: That is sitting down--
And facing a blank sheet of paper
White as if out of the Siberian snowfields.

2009

*Lev Loseff (1937-2009) was a Russian poet and friend of Joseph Brodsky.

** Joseph Brodsky wrote a poem titled, "Letters from the Ming Dynasty."

The Wild Great Wall

Here, stone gets its weight
Language acquires its silence
Even innocent death receives its dignity
And we the living, among the weeds
In a ray of the sun's dying light
Resemble a few wandering ghosts...

2012

For Imre Kertész

Between your words, fire and ice,
A convict's
Chains and freedom,
All creak and rustle.

In this country you've never visited,
The scenery is not all that different.
Already iron has grown into the land,
Poor children grow up eating icepicks for fun,
And beating on an empty jar from a past life,
When I read you
The echo comes back--
Yes, it was, and I'm afraid it will be
Our only music.

2012

Waking Up

Why did you wake up?
Because the light pierced my eyelids,
Because in my death I heard a bird sing,
(What kind of bird?)
Because I slept so long being so tired,
Because I heard the light tremble
On a tender branch tip,
Then came the dawn like molten steel...
Because I slept so long and so soundly
(As if I had been cursed)
Just to wake up in a foreign land
Where an unknown language almost brings me to tears.

August 31, 2013
Iowa

For a Future Reader

1

Not one poem I write this smoggy winter
Can match the memory of the sound
Of snow crunching underfoot in a pine wood.

2

Marina wrote with a goose quill pen,
But sometimes she did consider using an axe
As perhaps a better cure for her headaches.

3

Last night at the dinner table, Duo Duo said:
"Writing a poem means one less poem."
We don't understand the language of the dead,
Nor that of the living.

2013
Beijing

Ghost Ships

—for Robert Hass and Brenda Hillman

Outside Nanjing
The Yangtze River at night
On its ink-dark surface
Barge after barge sailed by
(Were they sand barges?)
No lights
No chugging motors
We said nothing
Unable to speak
As if Li Bai and his fellow poets knew we were there
Ghost ships gliding by in front of us without a sound...

August 2014
Nanjing

October Poem

While some poets in another world
Chant bronze poems of October,
I enter the only small park on our street;
No one walks with their bird, no one practices Tai Chi,
there's not a soul to be seen,
There's just an ash tree gasping in the smog;
The roses hang their heads like disgraced brides,
The gingko leaves fallen on the grass
Resemble dead butterflies that will never strive again.
Not a breeze stirs. Even the stones sweat.
Low-growing wild peaches huddle together
As if they alone still dreamed.
All of this seems to possesses an order of sorts--
The forlorn sound of the monotonous trimming
Has replaced all of the melodious birdsong.

October 2014
Beijing

Memories of London

A small garret room,
(Van Gogh's Wheatfield with Crows on the wall)
The quiet dining table in the kitchen downstairs
And a door that opened to the garden,
Even when no one was on the stairs
The sound of footsteps could still be heard
--that was East London twenty-two years ago,
You were thirty-five.
The others in the house had all gone home for Christmas,
Leaving you alone with the ghost.
Through the night you read a book about Sylvia Plath's death,
You wept writing letters home...
Then, then, one frosty morning,
When a glacier erupted in the garden outside,
You heard Bach for the first time.

2014
Beijing

For a Poet

There are no readers,
Or your readers just haven't arrived yet,
Or your readers are on a cruise ship in the Aegean--
A backpacker,
Hopping from one island to the next,*
Just chasing the light.

February 2015

* The Greeks call the tourists on the Aegean "Island hoppers".

Snow Poem

1

Dazzling white snow
A trail of footprints that turns back
Before reaching the center of the frozen lake

It's like a poem you never finished
At first you want to try, but later every step
Is accompanied by fear

2

Birds seem to like snowy days more than us
Passing through a little park
On a tall white poplar
I saw a flock of magpies hopping with joy
Eight of them

I posted the photo on WeChat
Someone said: "There's one more in your poem"

Yes, I'd forgotten all about it, but it was there

I have a stone heart
Also the heart of a magpie

I have a magpie heart
For which it's hard to find a mate

December 2016

Looking at an Old Photo

That was 1979,
Three years after the Cultural Revolution ended,
As a young poet, you visited the Old Summer Palace
Among the broken columns and stones,
Solemn looking, like one who's been suffering...
(Sorry, but now I find this this sort
of "memento" embarrassing.)

How many years it has been,
In Beijing, I rarely visit the Old Summer Palace,
Those ruins are no longer my own,
I've come to resemble someone
Who has struggled free of the stones; but
Sometimes I still think of walking there,
Especially on a frosty, snowy day
It's quiet there in the winter light
The burned stones are caressed by snow,
The sturdy trees are empty of leaves
And there are the cackling magpies,
The frozen ponds and the upside-down rowboats,
Walking there, I quietly think of
The desolation of my life,
Walking there, I no longer need
Anyone's company.

December 2016

Marginalia, 2016

*Destroy your manuscript, but save whatever you have
inscribed in the margin out of boredom, out of happiness,
and, as it were, in a dream.*
     —Osip Madelstam (The Egyptian Stamp)

Akhmatova

In the summer of 1941, Mars drew nigh above your roof,*
It wasn't until the winter of 2016 that I finally saw it.
Have the disasters passed? I'm not sure.
Only as the distance between us grows does reality reassert itself.

Pasternak

He wrote a poem in praise of the Great Leader
Afterward he was puzzled:
"Devil knows how that was written!"

Milosz

A wild rabbit fled before his headlights,
It ran along the bright beams of light;
You see, if I needed a philosophy,
It would be the kind
To help a little wild rabbit run away.

Mandelstam

Obsessively you hummed: "My age,
My beast;"
You looked for a reed flute
But in the end you pilfered
An axe from Sophocles.

Dante

It's not that you have an aquiline nose
But the eagle's talons under your brow, all the time urging you on

Wittgenstein

To what extent can a stone suffer
To what extent can we speak of a stone's pain
But is Mars not a suffering planet?
When a stone on Mars is in pain
Can you peacefully stroll beneath it?

Reading The Gulag Archipelago

Before some things are written about
Nobody would believe them.
Now we are talking, strolling and talking,
No fence comes between us
But rather a tangle of barbed wire

Szymborska

When she died she left a hundred drawers:
The various things she had used,

Collected postcards, cigarette lighters (she smoked)
Manuscripts, sewing kit, a model of Noah's Ark,
Passport, necklaces, Nobel prize diploma,
But one, when pulled open, was empty.

Koudelka's "Photos of Prague"

A watch on a wrist
Held out in front of a door or plaza steps,
History captured (12 o'clock, August 21, 1968).
But with no way to stop it.
Does that make you despair?
No answer. Amid steel and fire,
As a tank's turret turned, we heard
Only a click, followed by another...

Pound

You imagined pitching a tent at the foot of Mt Tai,
Passing a wondrous night of the soul,
And for me, I'd as soon be committed to your asylum,
Where I'd uh-huh and uh-huh
And others would think it was poetry.

Mayakovsky

You said you gave everything to the commune
Keeping only a toothbrush.
In fact, you also kept a bullet for yourself.

Camus

You said it was only in winter

You could feel an invincible spring on your body
When you said this
The dictators laughed loudly
They reached their fat hands toward the table
For another glass of wine...

Benjamin

You died on the road fleeing, you died on the border.
You died at the foot of the Pyrenees.
You died untranslatable.

Upon your death, a Jew
Hurriedly buried in a Catholic cemetery.
On the simple grave marker,
Walter Benjamin became "Benjamin Walter".
The locals said it was the only possible name they had.

Heidegger

Ultimately your black notebook confirmed
That a person is not loyal to a philosophy
Written while in a mountain sanatorium
But to his own blood.

Walcott

A great poet has departed,
Some read his poems, others write obituaries,
But I open an album of his paintings
There is a plurality of I's in his poetry,
And an abundance of eloquence, but in his paintings,
He shows us the shadows of trees in the heat,
And the parched stones...
He seems to observe with only his senses.

Suddenly the frame becomes a window,
With the sea since Homer
Surging toward me...

Eliot

April is the cruelest month,
So is August.
Many were the years you watched over your
Dry field walled in by stacked fieldstone,
While waiting for rain.
But your descendants all became nomads.

Young Zagajewski

Pray, pray
But he discovered he too could write prayers
(Even better than the ones at church!)
Pray and pray again
But he discovered he wanted more to praise
A girl with shiny lips and a pearl earring.
This was the moment he became a poet.
But as soon as he started to write this way,
He also discovered he had to bear
The dead's daily mockery of him.

Bonnefoy

We all know of Wang Wei's movement and stillness,
But what is the "motion and immobility of Douve?"**
The motion and immobility of Douve is a bow
Pulled taut at the edge of
Stone, snow, and conflagration

Bach's "The Art of the Fugue"

In this miserable world
We are accused of having such transcendent art,
But unable to resist listening,
I can scarcely hold back my tears, driving slowly
Where city meets countryside
Amid mountains of garbage and blank-eyed children,
Into my vast, impoverished country.

Beijing 2016

*In the third section of her Poem without a Hero, Akhmatova writes about the image of Mars. From ancient times, Mars has always been associated with the God of War. It is believed that when it draws near, various catastrophes will occur. 1940-1941 was a time of great conflict as the Second World War tragically continued.

**Du movemente et de l'immobilité de Douve is a collection of poetry by the French poet Yves Bonnefoy.

My Flight Path

(2024-2025)

Sleeping Beauty

—At the Met exhibition "Sleeping Beauties: Reawakening Fashion"

Sleeping Beauty, sleep.
We don't want to wake you.
In sleep you are at the height of beauty.
Lying there, your soul
Is beyond the range of any canon,
The folds of your dress are home to scurrying ants.
Your bloody dress smells of wheat fields, poppies
And rosemary.
Sleep, Sleeping Beauty,
Were you to awaken, you'd find
This is no longer your world,
That our vulgarity is unworthy of your beauty.
Sleep, sleep in the rusty furrows of the years
And beside the deep craters of fiery meteors
We can no longer fill,
A May breeze still blows,
Lifting the corners of your dress in a wheat field,
Where the butterflies of my childhood play.

September 2024
New York

Gwangju Boy

— On reading Han Kang's Human Acts

Gwangju boy
Brings tears to my eyes

Gwangju boys
Thrown in the back of an army truck
Their sticky blood
So many years later
Oozes still from your words

(How many young people really died?
It's still a mystery
A mystery to this very day)

Gwangju boys
Rotted in the soil years ago
Their parent's hair
Turned white years ago

Of the Gwangju boys, one
Was run over by an armored vehicle
Crushed beyond recognition

Faceless, nameless
He'll not appear on any memorial

But some say perhaps he didn't die
He was just "missing"
He was slapped by his grandma just
Before he skipped class to join the
       demonstration in town

That stinging slap

"One slap
Two slaps
Three slaps…"*

Is it you who holds
Your swollen cheeks

Is it you who keeps asking
Who killed our Gwangju boy?

But perhaps he didn't die
Because later he showed up alone
In a public square in another country
He was sighted with
Protesting students in Leipzig
Heading for Berlin, the Berlin Wall
Boarding a northbound train

After all these years, he is still so young
So impulsive
His eyes shine
With a young-animal glow
That brings us to tears

Perhaps he really is dead, dead forever
Along with our spring light
Summer rain and
Winter snow, all dead

Gwangju boy
Where are you?

October 2024

*The third chapter of Han Kang's Human Acts, which is titled "The Editor, 1985", tells the story of Eun-sook enduring seven slaps from her interrogator.

Flight Path

—for Jane Hirshfield

Switched planes at Tokyo Bay for New York,
      crossed the Bering Sea,
            then entered North American air space,
Amid the whoosh of the wings and the smoking trails,
I looked down and saw vast snow-covered mountains and glaciers...

A never-before-beheld spectacle,
The earth strangely cold...

"You're lucky, you took the polar route,
Otherwise you'd only see smoke filled sky.
Southern California, it's a nightmare--
The residents of Santa Monica have been evacuated,
Not far from where Brecht lived in exile, you know..."

O, Bertolt Brecht!
Fleeing from smoke to smoke.
As you anxiously gauged the blaze and wind direction,
We flew over Hokkaido to Alaska
As if returning to the ice age.
Taking an ice-cold Sapporo beer the JAL stewardess handed me,
I recalled Yasunari Kawabata's Snow Country,
Do you know how it ends?

It ends in a conflagration.

O, fire and ice.
The fire and ice of this world!

You're right, that Buddhist sutra you mentioned is startling--
"We live in a burning house."*
The liberated one comes from the snow country, offering himself to
the void.
The helpless offer prayers.
The eyes of the beholders, though high above the sky
Are scorched by flames.

No one is lucky.
No one can pull out their hair and go to heaven.
Tongues of fire lick all our homes,
The thick smoke seeks to suffocates us.
(The wild hare with a burned ear hopped into
A poem by Elizabeth Bishop.)**
And I lift my eyes again--
A half-naked glacier below the plane,
The white patch farther off is Greenland,
Almost the far side of the earth, on the edge
Of an imperial dream.
And I'm strapped in my seat.
And the firemen are under the waves of the fire
Running through the smoke.
Are your eyes also a conflagration?***
Must I write another marginal poem about glaciers?
My path forever seems to go
Through fire and ice.

January 25th, 2025
New York

* See chapter 3 of the Lotus Sutra.

**See Elizabeth Bishop's poem "The Armadillo".

***See Mu Dan's Eight Poems, 1, "Your Eyes Have Seen this Conflagration".

List of Chinese poem titles

这条街 (2016-2020)

这条街
从阿赫玛托娃的窗口
在威海, 有人向我问起诗人多多
来自张家口
一碗米饭
在你的房间里
黎明五点钟
告别
清明, 陪孩子去"扫墓"
一则传说
在圣托里尼岛上有一棵树
在流泪的队伍中
哈特·克莱恩钢琴
在老子故里
六月记事
凯尔泰斯·伊姆雷
在洞头
巫宁坤在1957
飞行
二月
仿小林一茶
一张纸条
放蜂人之死
致敬
野菊花
一棵桂花树
回忆西单白庙胡同11号中院

与此同时 (2021-2024)

旁注之诗, 2021
与此同时
在涪水河畔想起杜甫
遗言写作
"悲伤时代的伟大诗人"
2022, 重读米沃什

旁注之诗, 2016

我的航线 (2024-2025)

睡美人
——观大都会"睡美人: 重新唤醒的时尚"展览
光州少年
——读韩江《少年来了》
航线

About the Poet and Translator

Wang Jiaxin is a Chinese poet, essayist, and translator and has published more than forty books. His work has had an important influence on Chinese poetry and has been translated into many languages. His collection of poems in English is Darkening Mirror (Tebot Bach, 2017), translated by Diana Shi and George O'Connell, with a foreword by former US Poet Laureate Robert Hass. His poems have been published in The American Poetry Review, Words Without Borders, American Poets and The Kenyon Review, and he has been a poet-in-residence at the Dutch Literary Foundation (Amsterdam, 2022) and at the International Writing Program at the University of Iowa (2013). An esteemed translator of Yeats, Mandelstam, and especially of Paul Celan. He has won many domestic and international awards. John Crespi, Director of Asian Studies at Colgate University, has extolled his work: "Wang Jiaxin has exerted a far-reaching influence over contemporary Chinese poetry not just as a poet but also for his role as a critic and translator. Wang's poetic voice stands out for the gravity, clarity, and resolve with which it explores the individual's relation to history, destiny, cultural inheritance, and humanity." Wang Jiaxin was born in Hubei province and graduated from Wuhan University. He was a professor at Renmin University of China for years--he now spends most of his time in New York.

John Balcom is Professor Emeritus at the Monterey Institute of International Studies at Monterey. He is an award-winning translator of poetry, fiction, memoir, philosophy, and children's writing. Among his translations are individual collections of poetry by Lo Fu, Ya Hsien, Shang Qin, Wu Sheng, Xiang Yang, and Lin Hengtai. In addition to regularly teaching literary translation at Middlebury, he has also taught at the British Centre for Literary Translation Summer School and the Bread Loaf Translators' Conference. He is a past president of the American Literary Translators Association.

Books by

ARROWSMITH
PRESS

Girls by Oksana Zabuzhko

Bula Matari/Smasher of Rocks by Tom Sleigh

This Carrying Life by Maureen McLane

Cries of Animals Dying by Lawrence Ferlinghetti

Animals in Wartime by Matiop Wal

Divided Mind by George Scialabba

The Jinn by Amira El-Zein

Bergstein
edited by Askold Melnyczuk

Arrow Breaking Apart by Jason Shinder

Beyond Alchemy by Daniel Berrigan

Conscience, Consequence: Reflections on Father Daniel Berrigan
edited by Askold Melnyczuk

Ric's Progress by Donald Hall

Return To The Sea by Etnairis Rivera

The Kingdom of His Will by Catherine Parnell

Eight Notes from the Blue Angel by Marjana Savka

Fifty-Two by Melissa Green

Music In—And On—The Air by Lloyd Schwartz

Magpiety by Melissa Green

Reality Hunger by William Pierce

Soundings: On The Poetry of Melissa Green
edited by Sumita Chakraborty

The Corny Toys by Thomas Sayers Ellis

Black Ops by Martin Edmunds

Museum of Silence by Romeo Oriogun

City of Water by Mitch Manning

Passeggiate by Judith Baumel

Persephone Blues by Oksana Lutsyshyna

The Uncollected Delmore Schwartz
edited by Ben Mazer

The Light Outside by George Kovach

The Blood of San Gennaro by Scott Harney
edited by Megan Marshall

No Sign by Peter Balakian

Firebird by Kythe Heller

Salvage by Richard Kearney

In the Hour of War: Poetry From Ukraine
edited by Carolyn Forché and Ilya Kaminsky

A Crash Course in Molotov Cocktails: Poetry of Halyna Kruk
tr. by Amelia Glaser and Yuliya Ilchuk

Don't Close Your Eyes by Hanna Melnyczuk

Tiny Extravaganzas by Diane Mehta

Departures from Rilke by Steven Cramer

On the Road to Lviv by Christopher Merrill
tr. into Ukrainian by Nina Murray

Nothing Bad Has Ever Happened
A Bouquet to Victoria Amelina

The Farewell Light by Nidia Hernández

Downfall of the Straight Line by Charles O. Hartman

The God of Freedom by Yulia Musakovska
tr. Olena Jennings and the author

Away Away by Mark Pawlak

The Miró Worm and the Mysteries of Writing by Sven Birkerts

St. Matthew Passion by Gjertrud Schnackenberg

New and Selected Poems by Glyn Maxwell

A Precise Chaos by Jo-Ann Mort

Where Do You Live? by Jennifer Jean

Coming Ashore by Thomas O'Grady

Crimean Fig/ Qirim Inciri by Anastasia Levkova, ed.

The Scent of Man by Tadeusz Dąbrowski

Hungry Ghost by Bruce Smith

ARROWSMITH is named after the late William Arrowsmith, a renowned classics scholar, literary and film critic. General editor of thirty-three volumes of *The Greek Tragedy in New Translations*, he was also a brilliant translator of Eugenio Montale, Cesare Pavese, and others. Arrowsmith, who taught for years in Boston University's University Professors Program, championed not only the classics and the finest in contemporary literature, he was also passionate about the importance of recognizing the translator's role in bringing the original work to life in a new language.

Like the arrowsmith who turns his arrows straight and true, a wise person makes his character straight and true.

— Buddha